Six Figure Marketing Blueprint

8 Proven Tactics Small Business Owners Can Use to Generate up to $200K in Under 2 Years!

Stephanie L. Walters

Copyright © 2016 Stephanie L. Walters

All rights reserved.

ISBN: 153749452X
ISBN-13: 978-1537494524

DEDICATION

I dedicate this book to my family: Husband, Daughter, Mom, Dad and Sister. You all supported my zig zag path of entrepreneurship through the ups and downs. Thank you so very much!

CONTENTS

1. Our Story — 1
2. The Website — 8
3. Email Marketing — 27
4. Social Media — 38
5. Video Marketing — 48
6. Blogs & Articles — 57
7. Networking — 65
8. Text Messages — 74
9. Direct Mail — 86
10. Speaking Gigs — 98
11. Resources — 108

PLEASE NOTE

This book is slightly unconventional. It's double-spaced and includes note pages to allow you to write down your thoughts when creative ideas come up.

Links to all the resources listed in this book can be found at www.stephaniewalters.expert/6fresources

Enjoy!

1 OUR STORY

So it all started when I was 13 years old. I was assigned to cut the yard weekly because my dad had two jobs and didn't have time to do this anymore. I had to cut the yard once a week and would be paid $10.00. Man-o-man was I excited. Ten bucks to a 13-year-old in 1989 was a lot of money – I was rich!

Not too long afterwards I noticed something interesting. Whenever I would cut the grass and then water it the same week, the grass would grow faster.

BAM! That's it – I can cut the grass more than once a week and get more than $10. Oh man, I was one grass watering kid at that point. I would cut the yard at the beginning of the week, water it, then cut it again towards mid-week – so now I'm up to $20.00 per week. YES!

But wait, if I can cut it twice, why not three times a week? And there you have it, I had a business that grew three-fold from one customer. At thirteen I learned that you can grow your business, not by getting new customers, but by increasing the value of your current customer. Man, that would come in handy later down the line.

The next lesson – know your customer's payment tolerance. So my dad started looking at me with a side-eye when he had to pay me $30 a week. Yeah, I hit his limit!

Fast forward several years and I have had a number of attempts at owning a business and they all just didn't fit me and failed in some way. Thankfully that didn't stop me. Failure is OK, it's hard, but it's

OK. Why? Because with every misstep, there's a learning opportunity.

One misstep in particular was a desktop publishing business I started when I was a graduate student. This was back when people really didn't know how to use Microsoft Word and Excel like they do today. I was pretty good at using those programs, so why not start a business doing it? Yeah right!

The services included me typing up resumes, letters and some light data entry. I may have known how to do this stuff, but I quickly realized that it didn't mean that I needed to be in business doing. I hated every moment, which led to me turning the work in late or with silly mistakes. The lesson I learned – love what you do, or don't do it at all, the money is never worth the misery.

In 2004, I started a company that is now called

Mici's (pronounced mee-cees) Boutique. All of us, mom, dad and sister had different roles and responsibilities in the business. We started as an offline business that sold our products at craft shows and flea markets 40-45 weekends a year for the first two years. Understand, we all had full-time jobs during the week. Are you willing to hustle and give up your evenings and weekends for your business?

Once we built up our email list we decided to try out this internet thing, so we built a website, and signed up to send email blasts to the contact list. It was awesome! We could sell products without leaving our house – how cool is that! This led to our new sales and marketing strategy:

(1) Go to craft shows and flea markets to sell our product;

(2) Get them to sign up for our list;

(3) Give them a business card with our website address;

(4) Email them monthly to make sure they remember us.

So we trucked along doing this, but we hit a plateau in our internet sales. You see, we were selling products that you don't necessarily need to re-order every week or month. Knowing that, I started my search on what else we could do to get more people to the website. That's when I found Search Engine Optimization (SEO). SEO is how the search engines see and read your website; basically how to categorize it so that when people search for something, they know to show your website on the results list or not. It was really expensive to have someone do it for us, so I learned how to do it myself.

At this point, we had mastered selling to the public

(there's a book right there, because people are a trip!), building a website, the SEO, and staying in contact with our customers; we're rockin' now.

Fast-forward to 2006 and we see an opportunity to sell our #1 selling product on the wholesale market. We take the leap and call the company MB Distributors, Inc. We build the site, do the SEO and collect and send emails....and that's when it all came together! In the first year we grossed just over $25,000 and the next year......over $200,000 – OMG! Everything we learned from the boutique worked perfect for the wholesale business; I just couldn't believe it.

After that, a number of people would ask my parents (the face of each business) what we did to be successful. And in true fashion my parents would hand out my cell phone number and say 'talk to my daughter, she did it.' After a number of those calls, I created a marketing agency, Blue Top Marketing to help small businesses avoid the mistakes we made.

Here's a quick list of our mistakes:

- Not collecting emails at every event;
- Being slow to accept credit cards;
- Using an online design company for our business cards, post cards and flyers, instead of a local printer;
- Not having a real strategy to market and advertise the business(es).

So it is from the retail & wholesale businesses and the marketing agency that I based this book, to show you that you don't need to be an expert in the beginning and you don't need a whole lotta money either. Now that you know how we did, let's pick it a part so that you can do it too!

2 THE WEBSITE

I'm a big believer that your website is the center of your marketing strategy. If it's all jacked up, you're never going to get the conversions you need to keep your business running.

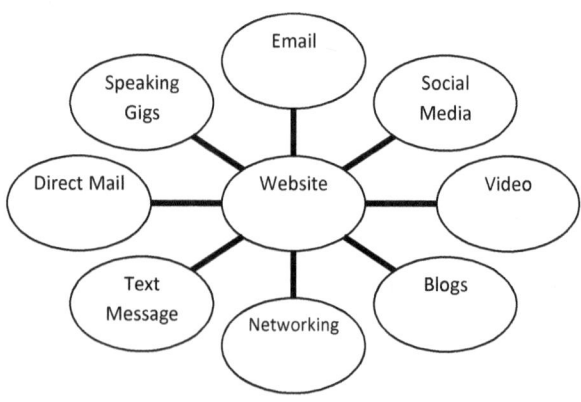

First things first, understand that your website doesn't need to cost $5,000 it just needs the basics and if that means that it cost you $100 to do, well, who cares?! This is not a competition, there's no prize to the person that out-spends on the building of their website. Personally, I learned how to build websites on Wordpress through trial and error. So I paid nil in money, but I paid a lot in time trying to figure stuff out.

With that being said, here are some basic elements that all websites need, with an explanation of why and how we implemented, and some resources to help.

Platform

We use Wordpress.org to build our sites. When we first started we used an e-commerce platform called Prostores, however they are no longer in business. Through Wordpress, we were able to pick the basic theme (and there are 100s of free themes available) and then load up our products and integrate all the other items on the list we're about to cover (called plugins). Wordpress is great because the platform is free and many of the plugins are free too. So you can build your site with a lot of flexibility without spending too much money.

You will go through your hosting company to build your website using Wordpress or some other platform.

Resources:

Wordpress.org

BlueHost.com (hosting)

GoDaddy.com (hosting)

Email Integration

There are a number of email platforms out there; we chose Constant Contact so that we could email people and conduct surveys. Whichever platform you choose, you need to make sure that people can sign up for your email list from your website. Here are some tips:

- Give them a reason to sign up, the hook;
    - "Save 15% off your next online order when you join our email club."
    - Free download of [yadda yadda] checklist when you sign up
- Make sure you have the sign up form on the homepage of the website, above the scroll line. People are lazy and may not scroll all the way down the page and see your sign-up form;

- Include the sign up form on all interior pages on the side. You gotta keep it in front of their face;
- When they sign up, make sure you send them a 'thank you' email.

How Implemented

We have an online sign up form on every page of the website. When they sign up they receive an immediate email giving them a coupon code worth 15% Off their online order. Then we send another email approximately 5 days later saying 'thank you' again with another 15% Off coupon, but a different code. So essentially they have two 15% off coupons to use, to get them back on the website to make a purchase (they could not combine the coupons).

Resource:

ConstantContact.com

Social Media Integration

Sign up for the various social media platforms that are out there, but make sure they make sense for your business. The best way to do that? Ask your customers where they hang out online, and based on their answers you'll know where to create accounts.

Once you create those accounts, you will want to include links to your profiles from your website. You've seen them at the top and bottom of various websites, you need this so that when people click them they go to your profile and 'like' or 'follow' you. This is another way for you to get your information in front of them and convert them.

Another option, based on your business would be to

include a live stream of your posts or tweets on your website. This gives the visitor a preview of the type of information you share online.

Lastly, for each page or product page (if selling a product) you want to include share buttons. These share buttons allow the visitor to your site the ability to share the information on that page with their friends on social media…digital word-of-mouth….you need this! The average person has just over 300 friends on Facebook. By offering a share button, you will now have access to that network.

Resources:

Facebook.com

Twitter.com

Instagram.com

Plus.Google.com

LinkedIn.com

Pinterest.com

YouTube.com

Payment Integration

Now days, it goes without saying, but back in 2006 we didn't think people would pay for our product online with a credit card…oh, but they did! If you're business can do it, do it. There are a number of payment gateway plugins available through the Wordpress platform. The cool piece is that you no longer have to go through a bank to process credit cards. Here are some tips:

- <u>Credit Cards.</u> In general, the credit card processors will charge on average 3% per transaction (some more, some less)
- <u>Shipping.</u> Will the customer pay it or will you pay

it? Either way, make sure to charge appropriately

- <u>Taxes.</u> Include this based on your state's rules
- <u>Upcharge.</u> We charged $0.50 - $1.00 upcharge to make sure the postage/shipping calculated correctly.

Resources:

Paypal.com (payment gateway and plugin)

Stripe.com (payment gateway and plugin)

WooCommerce (plugin)

Appointment Integration

When people visit your website and they see that you're the 'greatest thing since sliced bread' you need to give them a way to connect with you immediately before they leave the site. Appointment booking is a great way to get them right in the moment. We use it for the marketing agency and it works great. I know not all of you can use this, but if you can, do it!

Resource:

Appointy.com

Calendars/Events

Let people know where you're going to be, whether it's selling a product at a show or speaking at an event. Keep your fans updated on your whereabouts. We use this for the boutique when we attended various shows and for the marketing agency when I go out to speak to groups, have boot camps or host seminars. The resources for this are generally free.

Resources:

Timely (calendar plugin)

AJAX (calendar plugin)

Espresso (paid calendar plugin)

SEO

SEO stands for Search Engine Optimization. When the search engine robots read your site, they don't see all the pretty colors, they see raw data. Even though the text you have on each page, blog post or product page is data, it will take FOREVER for the search engines to find your site and index it. That's where Yoast comes in. It's a plugin that allows you to enter focused keywords for each page and blog post on your site so that the search engine robots know what to do with the information. They also can send a sitemap (all the data) to the robots to process in $1/10^{th}$ the time it would take them to find you.

Resources:

Yoast SEO (plugin)

Images* & Video

You need these. Your images should be hi-res and your videos should be short, under 3 minutes. For the retail and wholesale business we used stock photos on the product pages, and video on the retail site to show the proper way to care for the product. Additionally, we included a video in the 'thank you' email when people signed up for our email list.

Resources:

Picmonkey.com (free image creation and editing site)

Canva.com (free-ish image creation and editing site)

Animoto.com (video creation site)

Your phone (use your smartphone to record video

and load it up)

*Do not use images that you do not own or have permission to use

Service/Product Pages

Service: These pages need to be descriptive but not give away your process or secret sauce.

Product: These pages need to be written as if you're talking to that customer face-to-face so that they but it now.

Here are some tips:

- Get a copywriter to make sure you sound awesome (or a friend that can write really well)
- Use some of the wording from the manufacturer to create your product pages, but not the exact

words. The search engine robots don't like that.

- Give as much detail as possible on the product pages so that you leave no question unanswered.
- On the service page(s) include your phone number and your BOOK NOW button to give them the option to book an appointment.

Contact Us

Always have this page on your site – even though you included your phone number on practically every page, you still need this. Many people like to send you messages and/or questions through the site, and it is unlikely that they will copy your email address and go to Gmail, Yahoo, or whatever and send you an email with their question or comment. You gotta make it easy for people to contact you.

Mobile Friendly/Responsive

This is SUPER important! Most of the people that visit your site will do so from their mobile phone or device. Your site has to be responsive to this or the visitor will leave in less than 1 minute. And if they leave, you can't convert them, right? All the Wordpress themes are mobile friendly/responsive, but if you choose to go with another platform, make sure you check this before you get too deep into building your site.

Well, there you have it, the basics of building your website. You can check out all of my sites to see all of this in practice in some way.

www.stephaniewalters.expert

www.bluetopmarkting.com

www.mbdwholesale.com

www.shopmici.com

6 Figure Marketing Blueprint

Creative Juices: How can you use this for your business?

6 Figure Marketing Blueprint

Stephanie L. Walters

3 EMAIL

With all the new online marketing options out there, did you know email is still king? Yep, for every dollar you invest in email, you'll receive over $40 back. Based on that, you should never think that emailing your prospects or client list is a waste of time.

All of our businesses maintain an email list and send messages out on a regular basis. The only difference is the purpose and style of those emails. Let's look at some examples of when you can send an email to your lists:

- General Monthly Newsletter

- Holidays – real and any you make up on your own

- Major news events

- Events – self-hosted or you're attending

- Sales, Promotions

- New Product Announcement

Of these examples, most will tie back to your business or particular product or service. When it comes to the Holiday email, there are two versions:

(1) The promotion associated with the holiday – 'Labor Day Sale'

(2) The 'Happy XYZ' email

With the second version, you just say 'Happy Holidays' or 'Happy Labor Day' and don't include a promotion – just wishing them a happy holiday. Why? Because you don't want them to think that every time you send them an email, you're expecting them to buy from you. The less salesy you are, the more sales you will receive. Trust me.

Now let's talk design.

- Length. Don't make it too long. It is most likely that it's being read on a mobile device. If it's too long, people will close it before they get to the bottom.

- Call to Action. Place your call to action towards the top. If you bury it in text or towards the bottom of the email, they may not do what you want them to do. It goes back to the first bullet – they're reading it from their mobile, so you have to make it clear and upfront.

- Links. Don't fill up your email with a lot of links. Research has shown that the more links in your email, the less likely the reader will click on anything. Try to stick to 1 -2 at most.

- Pictures. You must have pictures. People are all about pictures – they rather read the text on a picture than just regular text. With that being said, make sure you give you're pictures a description, and here's why:

    o There are some people that are visually impaired and have screen readers. The screen readers cannot read an image, but they can read the description attached to an image. If you don't provide the description, the default text will be the file name of the image – who wants to hear about that?!

- o When the email arrives, many people have the settings of their cell phone to not allow the download of the image to save on data usage. As with the above reason, when this happens, the email system will display the file name. In both cases, you can change the description to meet your business needs.

- Social Media. Always include social share links at the top of your email. That way, the reader can share the information to their online network. Remember, the average Facebook user has over 300 friends in their network.

- Signature. You can use a regular signature, but if you're only sending your email once a month, you may want to include a headshot of the person most recognized with the business. I especially do this for Blue Top Marketing because I meet so many people at networking events, I want them to remember me when I send them an email.

When should I send my email? This is a question I get A LOT! My answer – I have no idea! What I can tell you is that the system that you're using to blast out those emails, should date and time stamp when each person opens the email. Scan through the list and you'll get a real sense of when people are opening them. Use that information as a guide and then just test and tweak.

Additionally, just know that if you're emailing consumers, it can take them up to three days to open your email. Which means that you will need to email your list the first time about an upcoming promotion about six days prior, and then again four days prior, the day before and then the day of the promotion.

Whereas with business emails, they will generally get opened within 48 hours. For Blue Top Marketing, Monday and Fridays were bad days to send emails to our business list. Plan your promotion schedule accordingly so that you get the biggest bang from your emails.

Resources:

Constantcontact.com

How Implemented:

- Mici's Boutique
    - Monthly email with a standard template format;
    - Holiday emails, if tied to a promotion or sale
- Blue Top Marketing
    - Automated email series to people that I met at networking events;
    - Automated email sent when we have a new blog post on our website.

Creative Juices: How can you use this for your business?

Stephanie L. Walters

6 Figure Marketing Blueprint

4 SOCIAL MEDIA

Oh how I LOVE social media! It has leveled the playing field between small businesses and big brands. You no longer have to spend $4 million dollars on a Super Bowl ad to get your message out to the masses. It allows you the same opportunity to reach your target market as any big brand in your industry. And, of course, social media gives you a chance to put a fence around your fans. Giving them a place to connect with you on a more personal level.

Remember when Facebook and Twitter showed

up on the scene and people just dismissed them? Fast-forward to today and you can't run a business without being on at least one social media platform.

Social media allows you to use online platforms to:

- Promote your services, events and/or products
- Pursue branding goals
- Increase market awareness
- Efficiently reach and engage with consumers
- Drive more business/increase sales

Why should you care? There are over 1 billion users on Facebook worldwide….yeah, 1 billion. And, the average American user spends 55 minutes on the platform every day.

I know some of you are going to say that social media is a waste of time and is completely unnecessary for my business. That you feel it's only for posting pics of food or family events or sharing random memes. Oh my friend, are you missing the boat on this one!

We were early adopters of social media, mainly Facebook and Twitter.

Resource:

Various social media platforms

How Implemented

Mici's Boutique

- Social Media link on our website
- Facebook and Twitter were linked together (I didn't know any better at the time – so don't do this!)
- We themed out the days:
    - Monday – Sheet color of the week
    - Tuesday – Product of the week
    - Wednesday – Promote an event

we're attending on the weekend
- Thursday – Random post
- Friday – Fun Fact, promote event we're attending on weekend
- Saturday – pics from the event we were attending

MB Distributors

- Social Media link on our website – only Facebook
- Posts to help our wholesalers market their business and sell the product

Blue Top Marketing

- Social Media link on our website
- Post the monthly eNewsletters
- Share tips and tricks from other sources
- Post or share events
- Pics from events or interesting people I

meet up with related to marketing

- Instagram: This account shows the behind the scenes of the business and fun random stuff
- LinkedIn: Keep very formal

You see, social media allows you to reach a large group of people that you would not have access to otherwise. But how did we get people to follow us?

At every craft show/flea market Mici's Boutique attended, we had a sign ASKING them to follow us. If they signed up for our email list, the social media links were included so that they could go out to those accounts and follow us.

With MB Distributors, we asked people to follow us when they placed their first order, and the social media links were included in the email blasts.

Lastly with Blue Top Marketing, I had the

information on the business card, listed in all my presentations, and in the email blasts.

I do have to say one thing about social media, specifically Facebook as of 2016. The golden days of free marketing on Facebook have long past. Though your business fan page is free and posting to it is free, to really get traction, you will need to utilize their ads feature to get the word out about your business (brand awareness) and/or product, service or event.

We have implemented an ad strategy in the last couple of years to reach more people outside of our usual customer networks. To make it work and to stretch your ad dollars, you really need to be clear about who's in your target is and what they look like (demographics). Male vs. Female, Age, Location, Interests, Behaviors, etc. Start by looking at your current paying customer base and determine your customer demographics from there.

Otherwise, Facebook is a great tool for reaching people, but you will have to have an advertising strategy to really get your content in front of the right people. This is also now true for Twitter and Instagram.

Creative Juices: How can you use this for your business?

Stephanie L. Walters

6 Figure Marketing Blueprint

5 VIDEO

We all know that Google is the #1 search engine, but did you know that YouTube is the second? That's just one of the reasons you should be doing video. Let's face it, people are lazy and don't really read anymore. Use that to your advantage and give them what they want – video.

Video has the ability to bring you more traffic, more engagement and better search engine ranking. You can do a video on practically every aspect of your business. Here are some of the ways that we use video and a few extra examples.

- Welcome Video – website, email signup
- How-To/Product Demo – website, YouTube, social media
- Give your elevator pitch
- Demonstrate Social Proof – these would be testimonials by your customers and clients
- Share tips and advice
- Answer questions
- Introduce your team
- Give a tour of your business
- Webinar – PowerPoint or you in front of the camera – website, YouTube
- Thank You – email, social media

The other reason you should be using video? It's great when mixed with social media. The same way people slow down to look at pictures, they will do the same for a video. The only caveat is that the video should be less than 2:30 minutes long. People do not have long attention spans anymore, so you have to work with that if you want to get your message out.

Each platform will have different rules on video, here's what I have found to work well:

- Facebook –2:30 minutes or less
- Facebook Live – 1:00 minute or less
- Twitter – 2:30 minutes or less
- Instagram – 60 seconds
- YouTube – 15:00 minutes

In some cases, you can create longer videos, you just have to know the attention span of your audience. Our audiences liked short bursts of information, so our videos were no longer than 1-minute for the retail business.

Blue Top Marketing on the other hand, has a

number of long videos that are seminars or instructional. They work well because the target audience is accustomed to 45 minute talks on a particular topic. But note that these videos are on YouTube and not shared on social media. Our social media videos stick to the 2:30 minutes or less format.

Here are some best practices to follow when utilizing video to market your business:

- Don't let perfection get in the way of progress!
- Use a good quality camera – doesn't have to be expensive
- Make sure the sound is good
- Be consistent
- Post the videos to YouTube, then embed them in your website

Video is really big now, so think outside the box to figure out how to best use it for your business.

Resources:

- YouTube
- Windows Movie Maker (editing software)

How Implemented

- Email –When people signup to our email list at Mici's Boutique, the welcome email has a welcome video inside.

- How-To – Blue Top Marketing has a number of how-to, step-by-step videos on YouTube or embedded on our website.

- Demonstration – Mici's Boutique created a video showing people how to properly take care of the particular brand of bed sheets we sell. That video is located on the product page.

- Sales – Blue Top Marketing uses video to sell the text message marketing service.

Creative Juices: How can you use this for your business?

6 Figure Marketing Blueprint

Stephanie L. Walters

6 BLOGS & ARTICLES

Writing blog posts and articles are a GREAT way to demonstrate your experience and knowledge as an expert. Whether the blog posts are on your own website or on others, this should absolutely be a tactic in your marketing strategy.

Most don't realize that if their website was built using Wordpress, that it is a blog site. That was the original intent of Wordpress, a blogging platform. So with that Wordpress site, you can just add a page called 'blog' and start posting to the site. To ensure that your information can be found, you'll use the Yoast SEO plugin we discussed in chapter one.

But what will I post about? A question I receive A LOT!

- Frequently asked questions (FAQs): what do people ask you over and over again? Each question can be its own post.
- What are you always explaining, or wish people knew before contacting you? There's another blog post.
- Step-by-Step instructions, but don't give away the store.
- Case Study – how you help your client achieve XYZ.

Here are some tips I have found to be helpful:

- Headline: Make it an attention grabber – don't be boring!

- Length: keep around 500-600 words. You will start to lose people once you cross this mark.
- Design: consider using bullets and/or highlighting sections. Many will skim the post, so help them out by emphasizing content areas.

Use the 'Publize' plugin within the Jetpack (for Wordpress users) to automatically post your new posts on social media.

Writing articles will have the same positive effect as the blog posts. Reach out to the publications that you subscribe to and ask to submit an article, just remember to not be salesy in the article or pushy in the request.

A great place to look for reporters that are looking for content is HARO, which stands for Help A

Reporter Out at helpareporter.com. They send out an email three times a day with reporter requests in various industries and topics.

Our marketing company has responded to a number of the requests and were picked up twice. Which is just another way to add credibility to your brand.

Other place to approach to write a blog post or article:

- Local chamber membership
- Local newspaper – yes, they do exist!
- Industry magazine
- Industry membership organization
- Professional networks

Minterest.com has a great list of places that accept blog post/articles.

When you're picked up by an external source for an interview, article or guest blog, be sure to share it with your email list, social media and especially in your media kit. It's all about showing that others see you as an expert – the ultimate stamp of credibility and authority.

Resources

- HARO

How Implemented

- Blogs – All of our businesses have posted blog posts covering various topics
- Articles – Blue Top Marketing had a number of articles written about the business, or we contributed tips/advice to articles through HARO

Creative Juices: How can you use this for your business?

6 Figure Marketing Blueprint

Stephanie L. Walters

7 NETWORKING

Networking has been a tried and true way to get the word out about your business and what you offer. I started networking in 2011 and it's been an interesting experience, to say the least.

When networking, the real goal should be to meet people, build a relationship and convert them to a client or a referral partner. The issue is that too many people try to do all of that when they first meet people at the networking event. Seriously!

This is what I have found to be the best and

efficient way to network:

- Attire: dress appropriately for the event. Just because you work from home, doesn't justify wearing yoga pants to the event.
- Business Card: the business card is not dead, and you need one when networking. Make sure it's descriptive of who you are, your contact information and what you do (use both sides to maximize space)
- Elevator Pitch: be able to say what you do, and for whom in less than 1 minute. Don't go on and on….please!
- Ask Questions & Listen: ask questions about the other person, both personal and business, and then really listen. It's all about them, not you.

Here's a list of Do's and Don'ts to networking:

Do: Attend a number of networking meetings

Don't: Attend so many that you don't get any work done.

Don't: Attend meetings that don't attract your target market. You want to make sure that you're hanging out with the right people either as prospects or referral partners.

Do: Bring business cards

Don't: Come without business cards. I have met so many people that arrive, talk with people and when asked for a card, they don't have one. Well, when I need your services in 3 months, how will I get in touch with you? If I run into someone that needs your services, how will I refer them to you?

Don't: Come with an old card that has a whole bunch of scratch outs and new information written on it. Business cards are really cheap now. Check out <u>Abbott's Printing</u>* – they have 1,000 cards, 1-sided, for $40.

Don't: Walk around just handing your business card out to every person. This is annoying and rude. Talk to people, build a relationship with them. It's through that relationship that they will remember you for future work and/or referral.

Abbott's Printing, South Holland, Il Phone: 708-339-6010 (tell I sent you!)

Do: Mingle and Chat

Don't: Come and sit and hope people come talk to you. It's networking, so you will need to stand up and walk over to someone and chat them up.

Don't: Try to get a signed contract at the meeting. This is a time to get to know people and build relationships. Don't be pushy and salesy!

Networking should be seen as drip advertising. You will see it working for you over time, but that requires you to attend the same meeting consistently.

Resources:

- Local Chamber
- Meetup.com
- Industry Association – or an association that represents your target market

How Implemented

At Blue Top Marketing, I attend a number of networking events. It has taken time to find good, quality groups.

Can't find a good networking event? Why not create your own?!

Creative Juices: How can you use this for your business?

Stephanie L. Walters

6 Figure Marketing Blueprint

8 TEXT MESSAGES

Text Messages? Yep, text messages are a great way to get the word out to your list and ensure that most of the people received it. You see, even though email is still king when looking at your marketing strategy, text message marketing can come in a strong second because there's a 97% open rate on those messages.

Now, let's be clear. We're not talking about texting people from your own personal cell phone – it's technically illegal to promote your business to your contacts in a group format, even though we've all seen it done.

Text Message Marketing works the same as email marketing. People sign up to be on the list, you send them messages with a link, they check out the link. It's all about getting people to your sales or event page (the link). A very simple, but powerful marketing tool because you're getting right into their pocket!

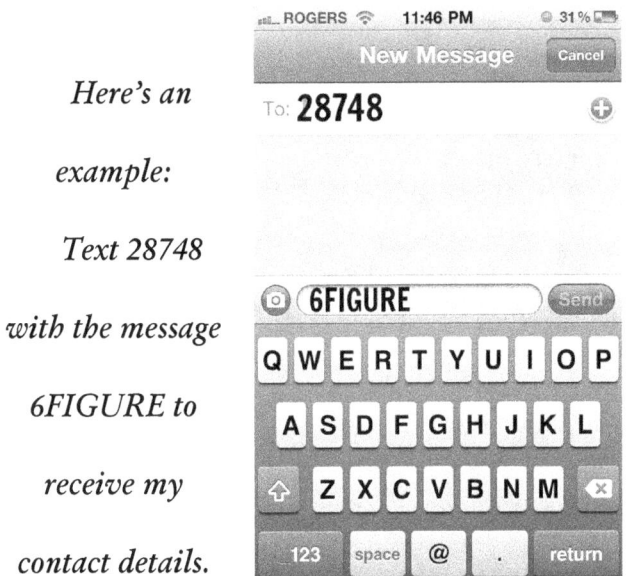

Here's an example:

Text 28748 with the message 6FIGURE to receive my contact details.

In this example, 28748 is called the shortcode and the 6FIGURE is considered the keyword. You segment your list using keywords and develop campaigns based on the demographics of the people on that list.

A number of people come to me and say 'text message marketing doesn't make sense or it won't work.' Here are some reasons you should consider using text message marketing:

   1. Relevant. Nearly 90% of Americans have mobile phones, over 70% say it's their number one most-used technology device and over 25% have ditched their home (land-line) phones.
   2. Engaging. 97% of all text messages are opened and within minutes of receipt.

3. Fresh. With over 70% of the emails sent being spam, text messages are a fresh, fairly new channel to push your message through.
4. Affordable. For as low as $40 per month you can push messages to 1,000s of people.
5. Easy. As an online platform, it's very easy to deploy campaigns that run automatically.
6. Build Relationships. Now that you can move your mobile phone number to any cell phone carrier, you can be confident that your messages are consistently received. (35% of email addresses change on a yearly basis)
7. Direct & Immediate. Of all the ways to contact someone, their cell phone number

is the best and most direct way to get in touch with them.

8. Automate. You can pre-write and schedule your text messages, run contests and surveys.

9. Trackable. By using a platform, you can see who opened and/or commented to your campaign. Include links and track them to view and measure the recipient's actions online.

10. Delivered. 20% of emails may not make it to the inbox, but with text messages you're practically guaranteed your message makes it through, with very rare exceptions.

With all of this information, how exactly can you use text message marketing for your business? Here are some ideas to get the creative juices flowing.

Texting Ideas:

- Appointment reminders. Before your doctor or dentist would send you a post card and/or call you to remind you of your appointment. Now, you can send a text reminder with a link to the office number in case they need to reschedule. Great to reduce the no-show rate by up to 50% or more.

- Coupons. These campaigns can reinvent this old-fashioned marketing tool. Send a campaign to drive repeat business, spread the world about a new product or service or to reward your loyal customers. These are more likely to redeemed because people don't have to carry them around in their purse, wallet or car and try to remember to use them.

- Voting & Contests. These are a great way to build rapport with your audience, and of course, get their contact information. You see this more and more with radio stations that run contests – keeps the calls to a minimum!
- Greetings. When someone signs up for your text list, you can have the system automatically then them a Thank You text along with a discount of some sort.

Resources

Check out videos by Blue Top Marketing at http://bluetopmarketing.com/text-message-marketing/

How Implemented

<u>Mici's Boutique</u>

We used text messages in a number of different ways for this business.

1. Events. We had separate list for Illinois and Indiana people that follow us at craft shows. That way we could send a text letting them know when and where we would be within that particular state.

2. Packing List. On the packing list of the items we shipped from online orders, we offered 20% off their next order is they joined the text list. We then sent text messages when we had major sales that led them back to the website for purchases.

3. Social Media. Every once in a while, we would post "Text XXXX to 28748 to join

our text club and save xx% on your next order." We didn't do this often because we didn't want to be too salesy on our Facebook and Twitter pages.

4. Direct Mail. Whenever we sent out post cards, we would give them a chance to join the text list, as well.

Blue Top Marketing

Here we created a special virtual business card that allowed people to obtain my contact information via text. Once on that list, I would send messages out just to stay in touch – no sales, no promotions – that included my email address for them to email me with a reply.

Because the messages come through text, it feels really personal and people either don't realize or totally forget that it's coming as a text blast.

Creative Juices: How can you use this for your business?

Stephanie L. Walters

6 Figure Marketing Blueprint

9 DIRECT MAIL

The basic definition of direct mail is a marketing effort that uses the mail (post office, FedEx, etc.) to deliver promotional pieces to your target market. Even though practically everything has been digitalized, direct mail can still have a place in your marketing strategy; it did with us.

What's cool about direct mail is that you have the opportunity to communicate directly with your audience, one-on-one. You can do this with brochures, catalogs, sales letters, postcards, etc. With us, post cards worked great.

Let's be clear, I did not hand write all the information on the front and back of these postcards. I had them created by a graphic artist and left space to write a person note on one side. Otherwise the core information was pre-printed. We also used real stamps so that they looked and felt more personal versus looking like bulk (junk) mail.

When designing your direct mail piece, look at the direct mail that you're currently getting and pay attention to the items that catch your attention. Save them so that you have a reference to go back to when you start working on your own direct mail piece. Also, make sure the colors you use are appropriate for the industry that you're targeting. Bright, wild colors may not work on bankers and lawyers, for example.

Once you have a design in mind, look for a

graphic artist to make it a reality. We were lucky enough to have a local printer that has a graphic designer in house. Another option would be to find an independent designer or check out www.fiverr.com and find a designer there.

When the direct mail piece is ready, send it over to your local printer and start the campaign. Be sure to track your results. If you sent out 1,000 pieces, how many people called, emailed, etc.? You must have a tracking system in place to know if the cost of the campaign is worth repeating, tweaking or dumping.

We have a call tracking sheet at Mici's Boutique and MB Distributors (they share the same business phone number) that we mark how they heard about us. We can track that new inquiry, and hopefully purchase, back to the campaign.

Lastly, we would call those that were part of the

prospecting campaign with MB Distributors to follow up – which switches the call from cold to warm. For Blue Top Marketing, the postcard worked in conjunction with an automated email series. That way, when they received the next email, they would remember me from the postcard and more likely open the email and engage with me in some way.

Resources

- Local Printer
- Fiverr.com

How Implemented

Mici's Boutique

- Birthdays – Once a month we sent out a 'happy birthday' card with a discount code for their next purchase.

- Christmas Holiday – In conjunction with our holiday email campaign to remind them to shop with us for their gifts.

- "We miss you" – Twice a year we would go

through our list and if a person had not purchased in six months, we would send out this postcard to entice them back.

- Testimonials – With every product shipped out, we would include a postcard for them to write a testimonial about the product. When received, we would email them a discount code as a thank you.

MB Distributors

- Prospecting for new customers – A couple times a year we would send out a postcard to all the independent furniture and mattress stores in states that we did not already have customers. By doing postcards we were noticed because other vendors sent out heavy catalogs or regular envelopes.

- New Products, Pricing – Any major updates to products and/or pricing, we sent it out by postcard and by email to our current customer base. This way if they missed the email, they still received the information.

Blue Top Marketing

- "Need a Speaker" – When starting out, I would send a postcard out the local chambers within a 100-mile radius of my office. This was moderately successful because no other speaker sent a postcard, they all sent speaker sheets in regular envelopes.

- "Great Meeting You" – Every week I would send out this postcard to the people that I met at the various networking or organizational meetings during that week. This is a great way to remind people of you (I included my headshot). This worked well because who's sending out personal messages in the mail anymore?!

BLUETOPMARKETING
Digital & Mobile Marketing Agency

Great Meeting You!

Social Media Marketing ~ Email Marketing ~ Text Message Marketing

From Bootcamps, Workshops, Webinars to One-on-One Consultations – We're here to spin you closer to your customer!

P: 708-808-0258 ~ W: www.BlueTopMarketing.com

SWalters@BlueTopMarketing.com

Stephanie Walters
BlueTopMarketing.com
430 E 162nd Street #359
South Holland, IL 60473

Creative Juices: How can you use this for your business?

Stephanie L. Walters

6 Figure Marketing Blueprint

10 SPEAKING GIGS

When I started Blue Top Marketing, the marketing agency, I REALLY did not like speaking in public. It horrified me. What put me over the hump of finally doing presentations? I would go to networking events and hear people speaking on my topic of marketing and would say to myself, "I know that information isn't not right," or "I can do a way better job than that."

And what's worse was that those people would get mobbed after the presentation and collect business cards and book appointments. At that point I said, 'screw it, I'm doing this' and I hosted my own event, a free seminar. Then over time I got better at it and became more comfortable in front of a crowd. Now, I can speak at the drop of a hat – you bring the stage and I'm there!

Now you're asking, 'how can I use this for my business?'

You have a lot of knowledge in that head of yours. You know stuff and how to do stuff that people want to know. Package it together into a presentation (no more than 45 minutes) and speak. Host your own events to start out and then branch out to local chambers, industry groups, etc.

Don't assume people don't want to hear what you have to say. They do. Just make sure it's not boring – they don't want to hear that!

Here are some tips:

- Look at your FAQs, can you do a presentation on one or a group of related items?
- What would you like people to know before they approach you or engage with your business? In general, or specifics?
- Have people come to you saying, "you should do a presentation/webinar/talk on that" – well, there's your sign.

I now LOVE speaking on various topics, but I had to get over my initial fear of public speaking, and practice in smaller venues to learn how to deliver information in my own style.

Resources:

- Do a search or create a Google Alert for 'call for speakers' (do this on Twitter too!)
- Check with all the organizations you're a member
- Check the national organizations of your target market to obtain local chapter contact information
- Really ---- tell people you're a speaker!

How Implemented

- My own hosted events.
    - Free Popup Q&A Seminars. People come register and come ask me any marketing question.
    - Lunch 'n Learn Seminars. They bring their own lunch and I bring

the 'learning'.

- Invited events.
    - Library. I reached out to my local library and developed a relationship with them to provide seminars to their attendees.
    - Chambers. I started with the chambers I had a membership with, and offered to speak at their luncheons.
    - Organizations. There were various business organizations that invited me to speak to their members or attendees.

The more experience I had under my belt, and the more people attended my sessions, the more people requested me to speak. Getting someone to refer you to an organization after they have heard you speak is gold…they're a living testimonial to your skills and ability.

Creative Juices: How can you use this for your business?

6 Figure Marketing Blueprint

Stephanie L. Walters

WHAT'S NEXT...

Hopefully you're ultimately excited to start implementing all those ideas you jotted down. I'm excited for you and can't wait to hear about your progress and success!

Overwhelmed? Well, don't be! Take one tactic, get it going, master it, then add the next one.

Head over to the private Facebook group created just for implementing business owners, just like you.

Keep in touch.

To your success!

RESOURCE MASTER LIST

Website

Wordpress.org

Bluehost.com (hosting)

GoDaddy.com (hosting)

Email

Constantcontact.com

Social Media

Facebook.com

Twitter.com

Instagram.com

Plus.Google.com

LinkedIn.com

Pinterest.com

YouTube.com

Payment Integration

Paypal.com

Stripe.com

WooCommerce

Appointment Booking

Appointy.com

Calendars

Timely (calendar plugin)

AJAX (calendar plugin)

Espresso (paid calendar plugin)

SEO

Yoast SEO (plugin)

Image & Video Creation and Editing

Pickmonkey.com

Canva.com

Aninoto.com (video creation site)

Windows Movie Maker

(program for simple editing)

Your Phone (capture video)

Video Hosting

YouTube.com

Publicity

HARO

Networking

Local Chamber

Meetup.com

Industry Associations

Text Message Marketing

www

Direct Mail

Local Printer

Fiverr.com

Speaking Gigs

Google Alerts

Member Organizations

National Organization in your target market

6 Figure Marketing Blueprint

ABOUT THE AUTHOR

Stephanie Walters is the leading marketing expert in the Chicago southland region. Stephanie is a "straight-shooter" who stays ahead of digital marketing trends and delivers laser focus techniques to crush the competition. Her marketing and social media workshops are often described as engaging "infotainment."

As a savvy marketing strategist, Stephanie created Blue Top Marketing to assist other small businesses grow their digital marketing presence. She engages clients through boot camps, conferences, webinars, workshops, individual/group strategy sessions, also known as a "Stephanie intervention."

Well-skilled in website management, Stephanie maintains a number of sites:
STEPHANIEWALTERS.EXPERT, BLUETOPMARKETING.COM, AND TSBR.TV, a newly developed television series created and hosted by Stephanie to help small business owners design actionable marketing strategies to grow their business.

www.ingramcontent.com/pod-product-compliance
Lightning Source LLC
Chambersburg PA
CBHW071820200526
45169CB00018B/488